Snozz

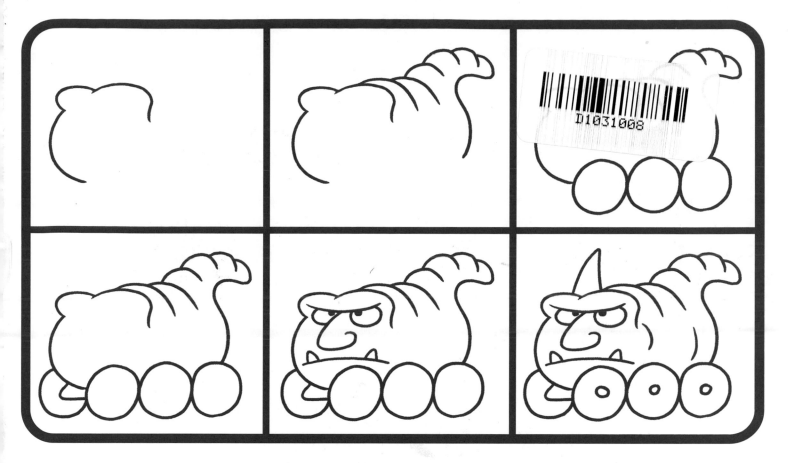

Gargoyle

Snorky

Gumph

Jarred

crab

Nessie

Matilda

Trog

Hairy

Eyeball

Sloppy

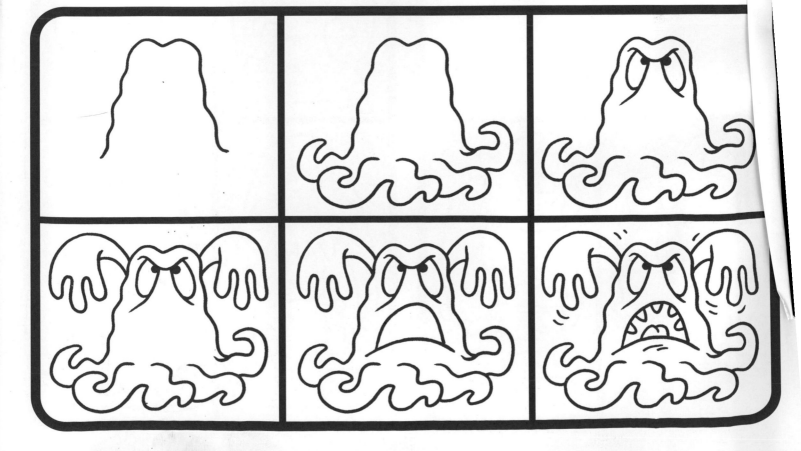

Eyeball

Sloppy

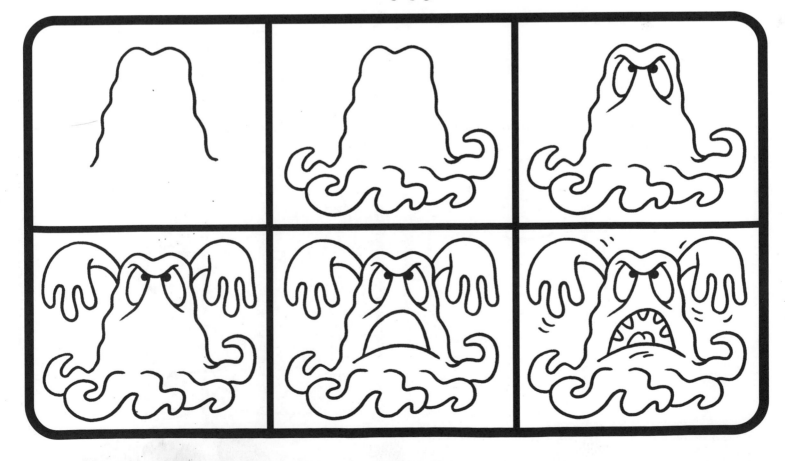

Trog   Hairy

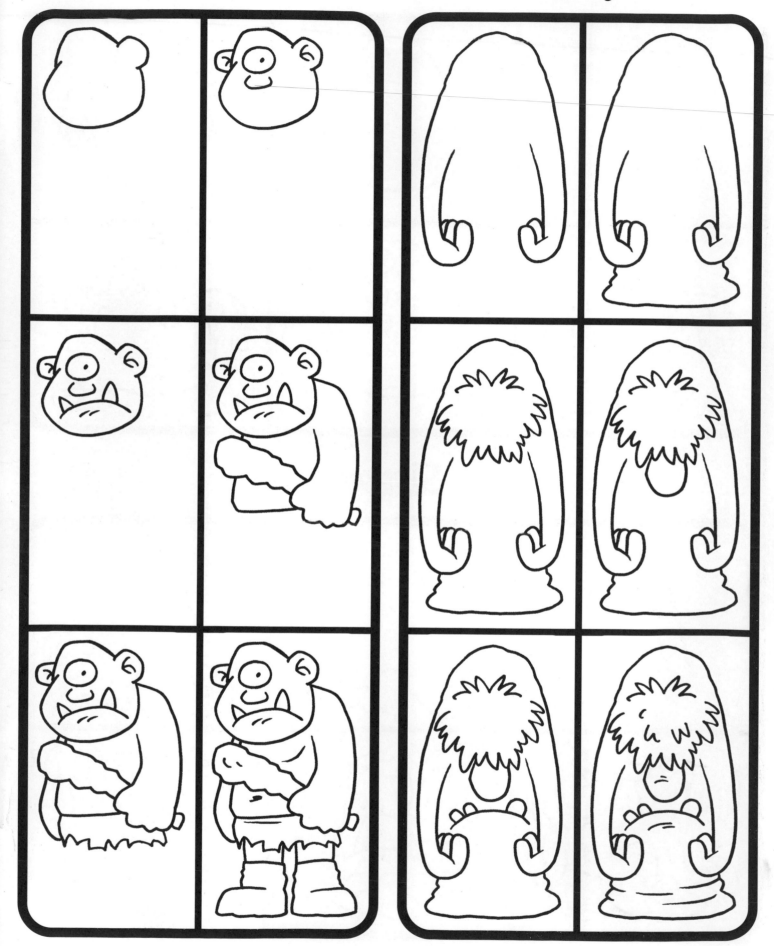

Medusa

Hag

Bull

Snout

Rough

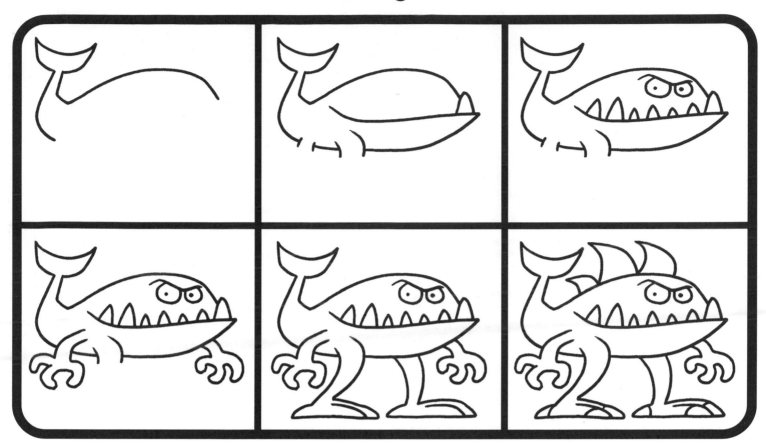

Troll-In-The-Box

Batty

Snurkle

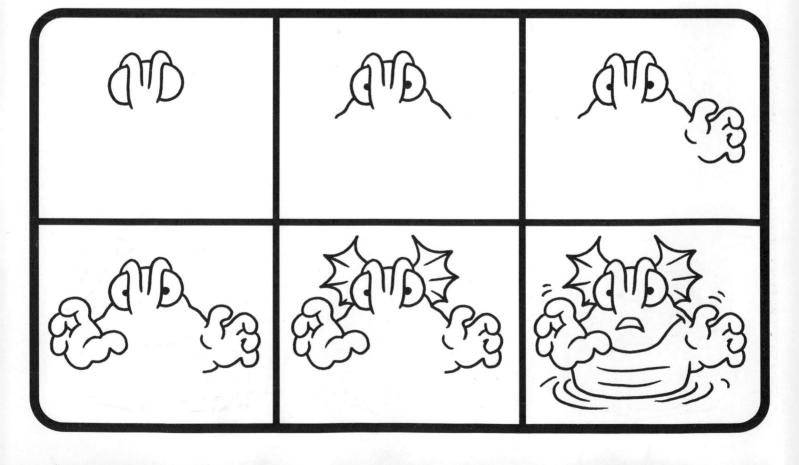

Mertle

Spider

Shaggy

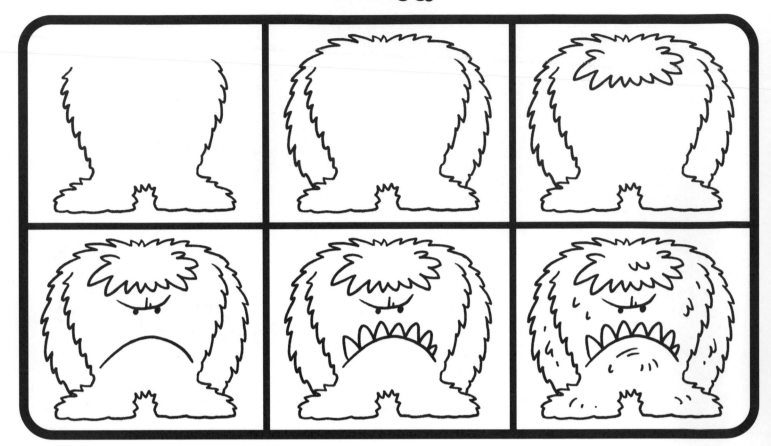

Wavy

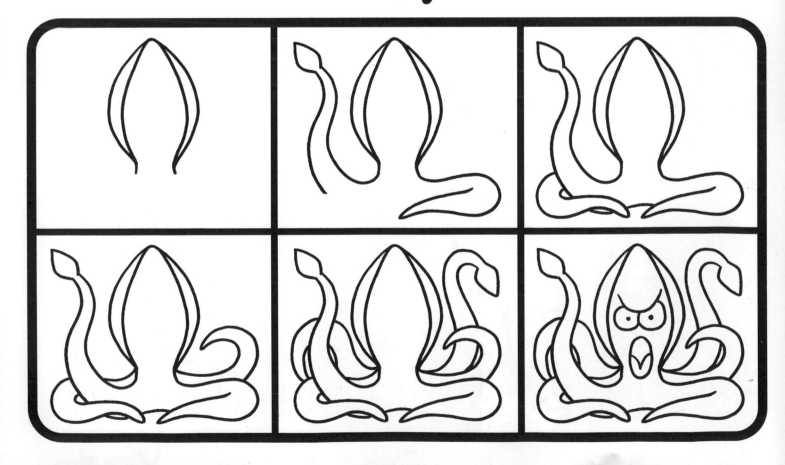

Pet

Vampire

Rah

Blob

Dev   Rock

Slimey

Slug

Flokk

Gumble

Warty

Dragon

Ted

Smelly

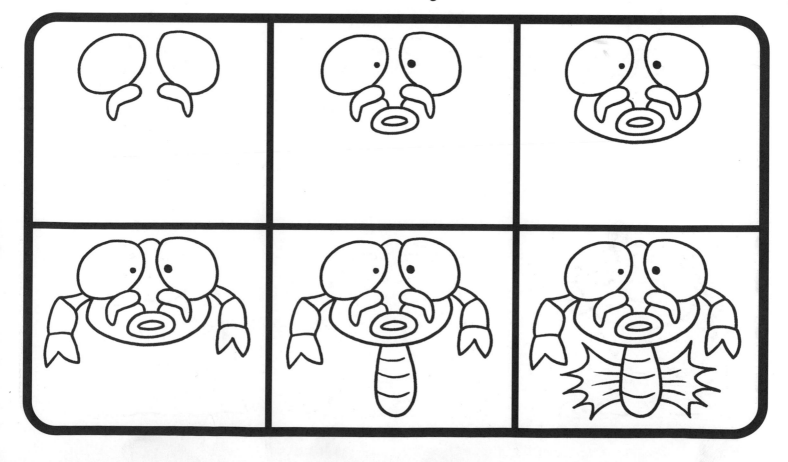

Colly

Nun

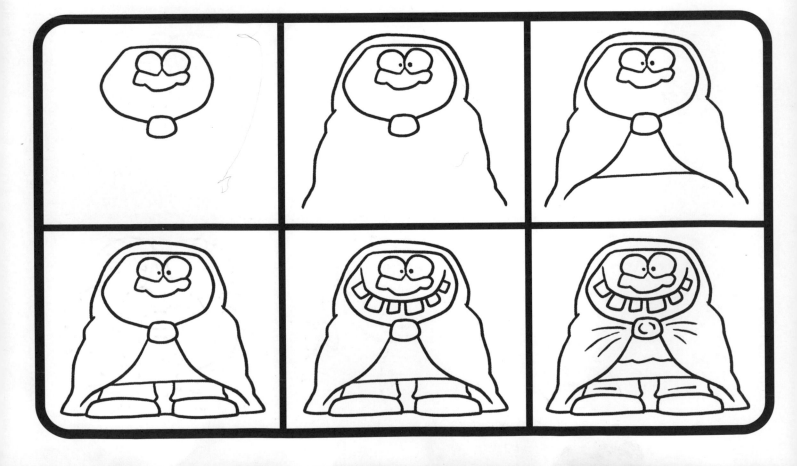

Sharky

Larry

Potty   # Verm

Horn   # Tree

Mad Monster

Mummy

Big one

Bendy

Eavesdrop

Squabble

Skull

Snail

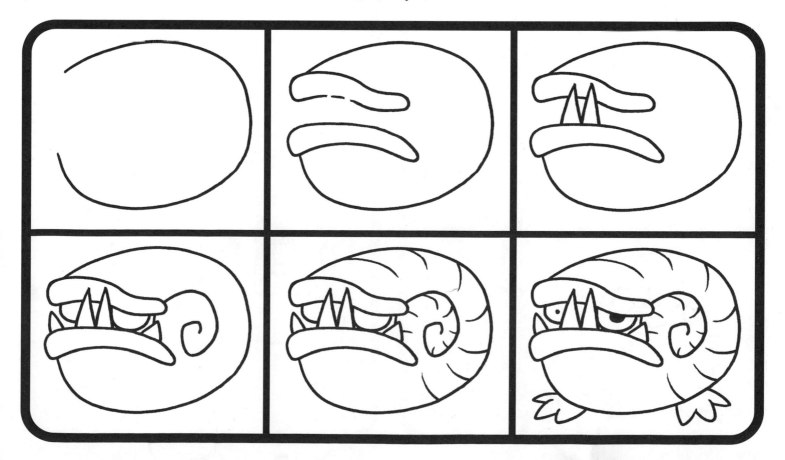

Rambo

Frankenstein

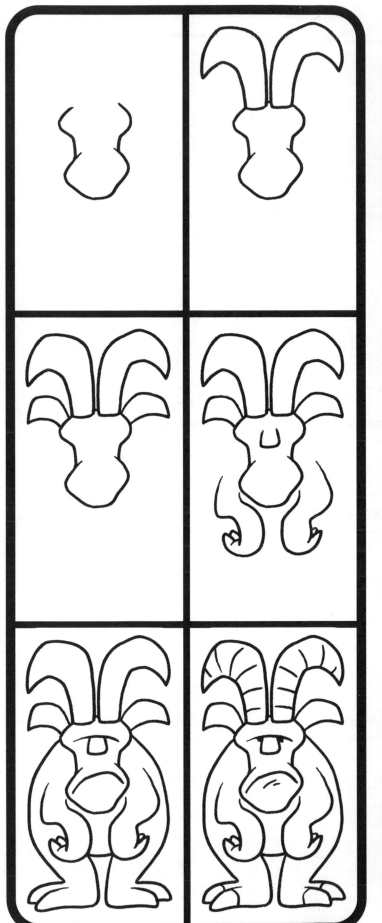

cyclops   Glum

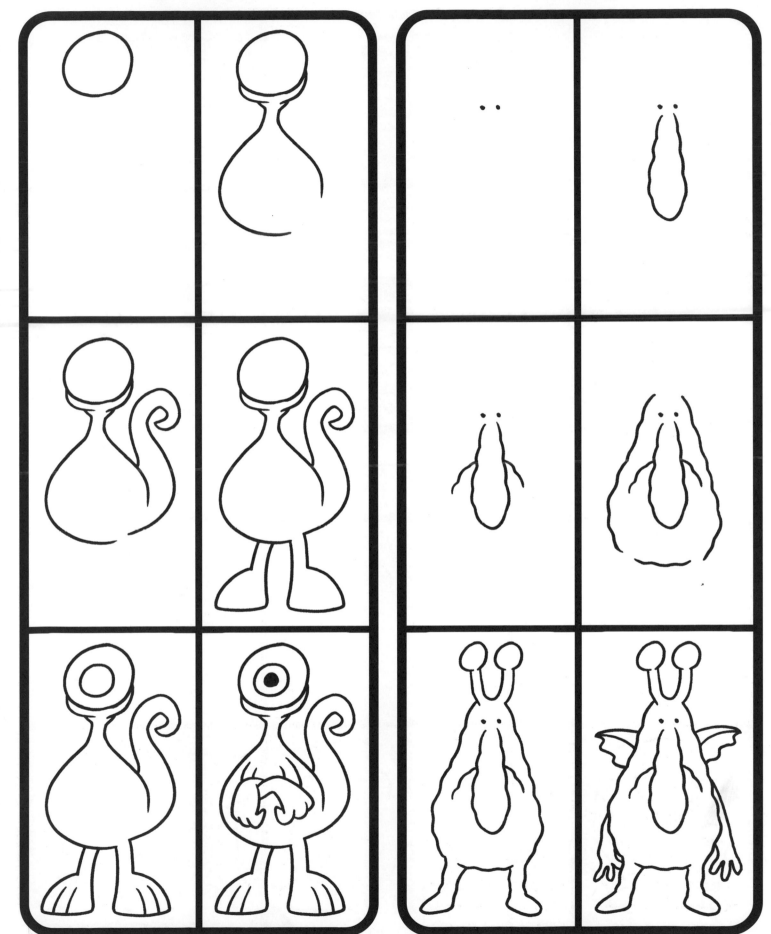

Scary

Witch

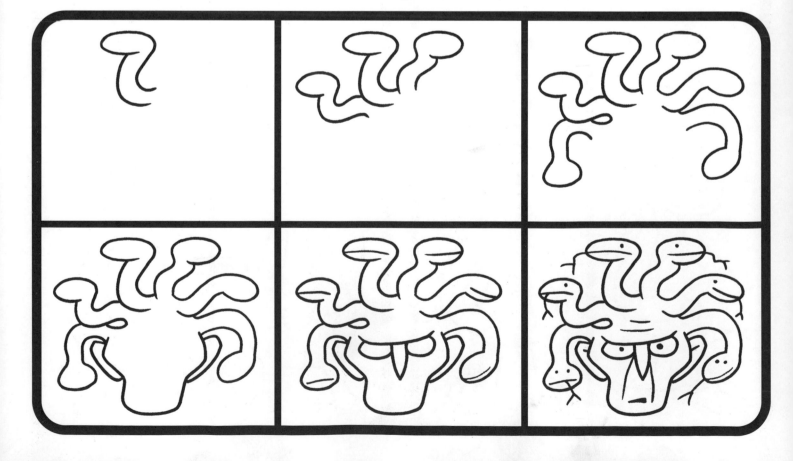

Jagged

Aaargh!

Troll

Bert

Hal

Nerd

cloaked Monster

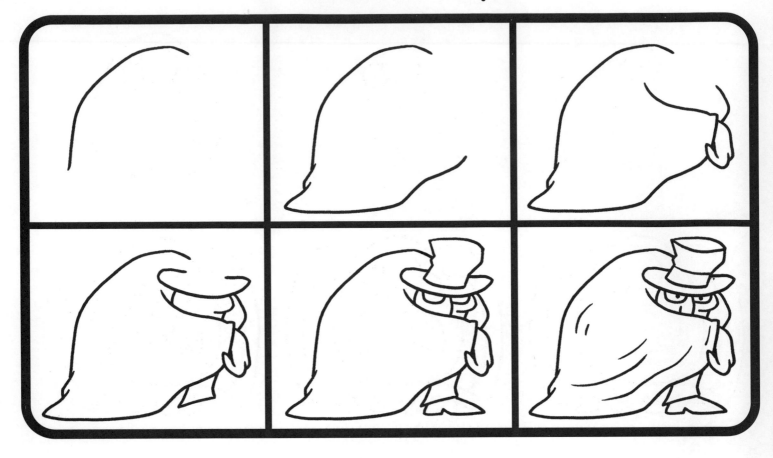

Squat

Werewolf

Robot

Lippy

Merlin

Granny   Grandad

Fingers

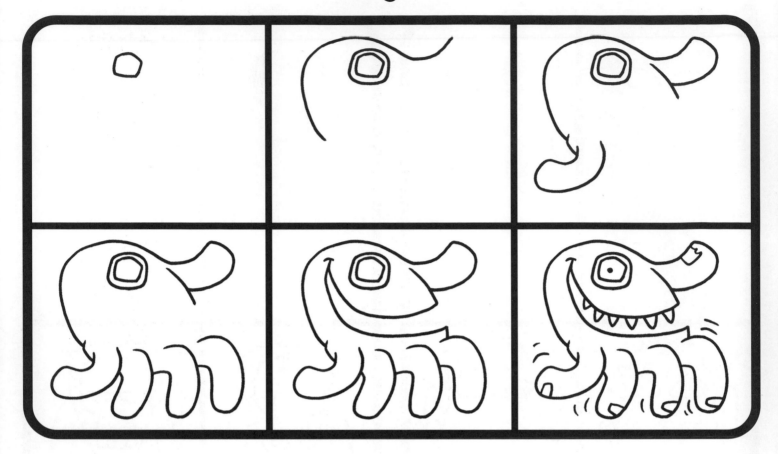

Pumpkin

Spot

Dalek

Baby

Happy

Growl

Wingding

Google   Johnny

Exterminate

Vanilla

Hattie

Bulldog

Venus flytrap

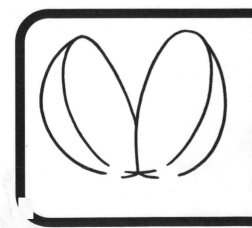

Slurp

Horned Beast

Big Mouth

Snorkel

Helmet

Herm

Beaky

Woo

Slump

Goggle Eyes

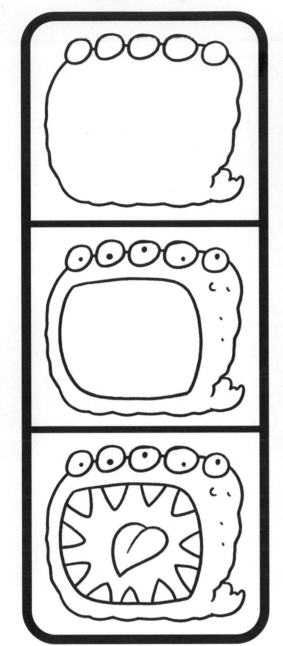

Truck

Slime